THE COLUMBUS ENCOUNTER
A Multicultural View

by Rosemary Tweet and Marsie Habib

Self-directed study units for grades K–3 and 4–8, gifted.
Easily adaptable for regular classroom use.

Interdisciplinary and product-oriented through the use of:

> Evaluating
>
> Classifying
>
> Comparing
>
> Imagining
>
> Researching
>
> Creating
>
> Reporting
>
> Mapping and Charting
>
> Thinking and Reacting
>
> Career Exploration

ZEPHYR PRESS
Tucson, Arizona

*We would like to extend special thanks to
Michael Habib, Lyle Tweet, Steve Tweet, Marcelete Elter,
Norma Horswell, Susan Pease, and Kathy Short.*

The Columbus Encounter
A Multicultural View

Grades K–8

© copyright 1992 Zephyr Press

ISBN 0-913705-77-2

Editors: Stacey Lynn and Stacey Shropshire
Book Design, Illustration and Production: Nancy Taylor

Zephyr Press
P.O. 13448
Tucson, Arizona 85732-3448

BK $22.00

CONTENTS

The Premise IV

Teacher's Section

    A Word to the Teacher 1

    Rationale for Self-directed Learning 3

    From Passive Learner to Active Participant 5

    The Format 6

    Suggested Readings 7

    Getting Started 8

    Interest Development Center 9

    Columbus Web 10

    Time Line 11

    Teacher Demonstration: How a Globe Becomes a Map 12

Student Units

    Unit I: Kindergarten through Grade Three 15

        Part A: Who "Discovered" America? 16

        Part B: About Columbus 20

        Part C: The World in 1492 26

        Part D: Explorations of the 1400s and 1500s 32

        Part E: 500 Years of Change 34

    Unit II: Grades Four through Eight 37

        Part A: Who "Discovered" America? 38

        Part B: About Columbus 40

        Part C: The World In 1492 50

        Part D: Explorations of the 1400s and 1500s 62

        Part E: 500 Years of Change 66

Exploring the Arts 73

Crossword Key 83

Bibliography 84

THE PREMISE

◆ *Learning Is Natural* ◆

Children are active participants in their learning, not passive vessels to be filled.

They are always seeking and choosing what they will learn and what they will not learn.

Their interest, trust, and active involvement is crucial.

Children tend to become personally involved in projects that appeal to a variety of modalities . . . reading, writing, reasoning, building, imagining, and creating.

What a gift we give when we respect the child's natural need to explore, to reflect, to communicate, to dream, to celebrate!

(Available in poster form from Zephyr Press)

A WORD TO THE TEACHER
The Columbus Controversy

*Human history becomes more and more a race between
education and catastrophe. —H. G. Wells*

This study is a look at the tumultuous joining of two worlds: Europe, Asia, and Africa with North and South America. Goals of the unit include the following:

◆ **To invite students to explore the meaning of the word *culture*** and how culture affects the outlook and everyday life of all individuals. Culture forms a framework of similarities within a group. However, within that same group are countless individual viewpoints. To imply that everyone within a culture thinks and behaves in the same manner without also pointing out the uniqueness of the individuals is to teach cultural stereotypes.

◆ **To invite students to explore early peoples and visitors to the Americas.** Two questions considered here are (1) Who lived in the Americas before Columbus's voyages? and (2) Who might have visited the Americas before Columbus?

◆ **To invite students to explore the impact of the cultural exchange that took place between the Old World and the Americas.** Europeans and Native Americans had extremely different cultural outlooks. Europeans taught many positive things to the Native Americans and vice versa. However, Native Americans were also subjected to the greed, intolerance, and disease of the Europeans. For Europeans and others from the Old World, land ownership was the norm, but Native Americans did not consider the land ownable. Europeans also had ravaging weapons of war and came from the horrifying times of the Inquisition, when persecution was the norm. Besides committing overt acts of terror, they also caused thousands of deaths by inadvertently bringing diseases to the Americas from the Old World.

◆ **To invite students to explore the life and legacy of Christopher Columbus.** This study has been written to help students view Columbus within the context of his times, neither to deify nor defile him. However, this study goes beyond what is traditionally taught about Columbus. Usually the story stops when he steps off the ship onto the island in the Caribbean. This view omits the next twelve years and the next three voyages. See the biography of Columbus in Unit II for further information.

◆ **To invite students to understand that history is subjective.**
In retelling the story of Columbus, most authors writing for
American schools have been of European heritage, resulting in
a Eurocentric viewpoint. In particular, the Native American viewpoint is often eliminated, partly because it contains atrocities
committed against native groups.

However, much can be told about Native Americans without dwell-
ing on the violence. This might include the diverse cultures of the
Caribbean islands and the Americas when Columbus arrived; the
advanced knowledge of the Incas and Aztecs; the unfairness and
cruelty to which the Europeans subjected the native peoples (without the graphic descriptions or drawings); and the multitude of
gifts that the Native Americans gave to the Old World. Many
aspects of the Native American culture can and should be taught
along with the story of Columbus, since the two collided to change
the world forever.

◆ **To invite students to understand the world as it was in the
1440s–1500s.** The more complete the story of Columbus's times,
the more students will see that he was a complex man living in a
complex period of history.

To achieve these broad goals, five sections make up this study:

- ◆ Who "Discovered" America?
- ◆ About Columbus
- ◆ The World in 1492
- ◆ Explorations of the 1400s and 1500s
- ◆ 500 Years of Change

It is recommended that all units be covered, since studying Columbus out
of context tends to give a distorted view of history. It is difficult to tell the
whole story in a classroom, partly because most children's books on Columbus either stop at the first landing or refer to Native Americans as ignorant
heathens. We have recommended books for each section, but you may want
to use other books that you think are appropriate. If you have books that are
obviously biased, you might use them to teach the cultural or personal viewpoint.

RATIONALE FOR
SELF-DIRECTED LEARNING

Our children's education must be more than the memorization of capitals of the states, the products of countries, and dates and places of past wars. Most teachers and parents would agree that what is also wanted is for our children to learn to think for themselves, to organize their own time, to make wise choices, to work independently, and to thoughtfully evaluate the results of their study.

OBSTACLES TO INDEPENDENT LEARNING

In spite of the teacher's best efforts, many, if not most, classroom programs involve students in schedules and organizational plans that foster dependence rather than the independence we prefer. Students are told what is to be learned and how long it will take them to learn it. The teacher not only defines the resources but also decides whether the learning experience was a satisfactory and valuable one.

A LEARNING ATMOSPHERE

Each time we, as educators, focus on what our objectives are, we need to take a fresh look at our classroom mode of operation and evaluate the effectiveness of the way we teach. Quite naturally, for most of us, our teaching style has had more to do with how we were taught than with what recent research has shown about the learning process. Even our good instincts have been overcome by the years of conditioning we have known in our own educational process.

Like a breath of fresh air, recent findings from research on the brain support our intuitive knowledge. This research shows that our brains are receptive to learning only under certain conditions. Our job is to translate that information into a classroom atmosphere that provides

- ◆ challenge
- ◆ freedom within structure
- ◆ trust and warmth
- ◆ opportunities to experience success
- ◆ personal involvement in the curriculum

A natural transition generally occurs that transforms the former "teacher-lecturer" into a "fellow learner." As fellow learner, the teacher becomes a resource person, a facilitator, and a classroom manager. In this maturing atmosphere, students gradually come to see themselves as responsible for their own learning, and a foundation for self-direction is set.

At this point, an unexpected problem sometimes arises. We find students no more ready for their independent learning than we, as teachers, were ready to allow it. This common occurrence is mentioned repeatedly in the literature dealing with programming for the gifted, an area in which independent study and research are recommended as major curricular activities. See Suggested Readings: Maker (1982) and Feldhusen and Treffinger (1980).

FROM PASSIVE LEARNER TO ACTIVE PARTICIPANT
Bridging the Gap

The Zephyr self-directed study unit was developed expressly to bridge that gap: to transport the student from the position of passive recipient to that of an active participant in his/her own pursuit of knowledge.

Within the defined structure of each unit, the students are given opportunities to

- make choices
- learn at their own pace
- learn in a manner suited to their own learning style
- expand their research skills
- use a variety of modalities
- plan their own time
- develop the skills of creative, critical, and evaluative thinking
- experience whole-brain learning

Because assuming responsibility for directing their own learning is often an unfamiliar situation for students, they will need your encouragement at the start. Generally within six to nine weeks most students will be well on their way from teacher-dependence to self-motivation. (Beginning the venture with only a few choices, then gradually arranging the setting so that there are more and more choices works best.) As students assume more responsibility, many teachers begin to consider the school library as just another part of the classroom. The benefits are many, from gaining a personal relationship with the librarian to learning about the enormous resources available in most school libraries.

Eventually, a few students will be ready for a true investigative research study of professional quality as suggested by Joseph Renzulli in *Enrichment Triad Model: A Guide for Developing Defensible Programs for the Gifted and Talented*, 1977.

THE FORMAT

Originally developed for gifted students, these units emphasize the use of higher-level thinking skills and are appropriate for use in any classroom where the goal is to encourage students to become responsible for their own education.

Interdisciplinary in content, each unit envelops a broad view of the topic by integrating the "basics" into each activity.

Within this book are two complete units: one created for the lower elementary gifted student and one for the upper elementary gifted student. Suggestions for adapting or adjusting either of the levels to fit any individual classroom are included.

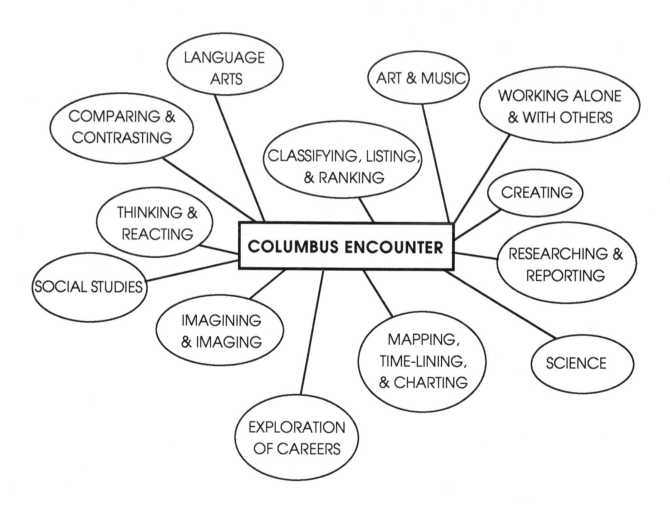

SUGGESTED READINGS
Self-directed Study

Barbe, W., and J. Renzulli. *Psychology and Education of the Gifted*. New York: Irvington Publications, 1982.

Brewer, Chris, and Don G. Campbell. *Rhythms of Learning: Creative Tools for Developing Lifelong Skills*. Tucson, Ariz.: Zephyr Press, 1991.

Clark, B. *Growing Up Gifted*. Columbus, Ohio: Merrill Publishing Company, 1988.

Feldhusen and Treffinger. *Creative Thinking and Problem Solving in Gifted Education*. Dubuque, Iowa: Kendall-Hunt Publishing, 1980.

Maker, C. J. *Curriculum Development for the Gifted*. Rockville, Md.: Aspen Systems Corporation, 1982.

Malehorn, H. *Open to Change: Options for Teaching Self-directed Learners*. Palo Alto, Calif.: Scott Foresman Company, 1978.

Purkey, W. W. *Inviting School Success: A Self-Concept Approach to Teaching and Learning*. Belmont, Calif.: Wadsworth Publishing Company, Inc., 1978.

Renzulli, J. *Enrichment Triad Model: A Guide for Developing Defensible Programs for the Gifted and Talented*. Mansfield, Conn.: Creative Learning Press, 1977.

Udall, Anne J., and Joan E. Daniels. *Creating the Thoughtful Classroom: Strategies to Promote Student Thinking*. Tucson, Ariz.: Zephyr Press, 1991.

GETTING STARTED

1. Select a topic as an extension of a regular subject (particularly when your class seems to crave more), or select a topic to pursue that is of particular interest and may not be a part of the curriculum. To zero in on special interests, administer an interest survey to each student.

2. Copy the unit for each student. When using these units for the entire class, you may want to expand or delete activities for individual students.

3. Set up a center in the classroom that encourages exploration in the subject field. You'll want to include a variety of materials. Be creative—the purpose of the center is to excite the students, so begin with lots of hands-on materials. Allow for ample browsing time and encourage students to investigate and become absorbed.

4. Go over each activity in the unit with the students, discussing and answering any questions. You as teacher are the key to successful implementation. Because most children are already well versed in the "One Right Answer" game, they will need encouragement to branch out into many of the open-ended activities in the packets.

5. Set the stage. Plan conferences and provide resources as needed. Then, get out of the way and let your students learn.

6. Give as much time as each student needs to complete each activity in the unit. The entire packet might take from five to ten weeks or longer.

7. As each activity is completed and evaluated, initial the activity near each number. You will want to evaluate on the basis of the response that is appropriate for each individual student.

8. When a student shows extreme interest in the topic, the completion of this unit might be only the beginning. This student may be ready for further study and research and may need only resources, guidance, and freedom to pursue his/her well-planned project.

INTEREST DEVELOPMENT CENTER
The Columbus Encounter

BOOKS, VIDEOS, FILMSTRIPS, FILM LOOPS, POSTERS ABOUT:

The "discovery" of America
Early astronomy
The Age of Exploration, 1400–1550
Navigation
Christopher Columbus
The Columbus controversy
Native Americans today
Early Native Americans: Incas, Aztecs, and Mound Builders
Native American art
The European Renaissance
Marco Polo and his travels
The Orient and Africa in the early 1500s

MAPS

A globe
Peters' map from UNICEF
Atlas of world
Historical atlases
Old World and other world maps
Earth's features from space

ARTIFACTS

Replicas of ships of 1500s
Native American clothing
Silk
Native American art—sculpture, pottery,
   weaving, beadwork, jewelry, carving
Spices—nutmeg, cloves, cinnamon
   in whole form

CHARTS

Time line of world civilizations
Time line of world exploration
Columbus's four voyages
The Americas' civilizations in 1492

PICTURES

Renaissance paintings showing
   clothing, daily life, great artists'
   works
Chinese art
Indonesian art
Mayan buildings

MUSIC

Native American
Sounds of the rain forest
Peruvian
Sounds of the sea
African
Renaissance
Chinese
Indonesian

TO PREPARE FOR FURTHER RESEARCH, STUDENTS WILL NEED TO DECIDE:

◆ What will the study be? What will be investigated and produced?

◆ Where will the background information be found (e.g., speaker, interviews, books, film, microfiche, documents)?

◆ What, exactly, will be the form of the product: a model, a manuscript, or . . . ?

◆ Who might be interested in the product: professionals in the field, publishers, organizations . . . ?

◆ What is needed to begin: specific plans, resources, deadlines . . . ?

SUGGESTIONS FOR ADAPTING THE UNIT TO YOUR PARTICULAR LEARNING SITUATION

◆ Require fewer, or more, research sources.

◆ Assign more of the activities to small groups instead of to individual students.

◆ Give fewer or more choices.

◆ Delete some activities altogether.

◆ Arrange the unit as a class project with students choosing different parts to complete.

◆ Add some activities of your own.

COLUMBUS WEB

The following web or mind map provides a visual way to organize possible topics of study. Students will have greater ownership if you web the topic with them, putting Columbus in the center of a large sheet of paper and letting the students brainstorm associations, categories, and facts. Even the youngest students can follow this group process, but their final web will be less complex.

It is not necessary that students come up with all that is included in the sample web, and students may come up with topics not on the sample web. The web may be left up as it is, or while the students work through the unit they may add new topics. A different colored marker could differentiate between their first thoughts and thoughts developed throughout the study.

The questions and projects in this book are intended to give students several selections to choose from. Students working individually or in small groups will have the opportunity to share at the World Fair and Feast (see page 73 in the Exploring the Arts section). Students will have a chance to learn from their own research as well as that of others.

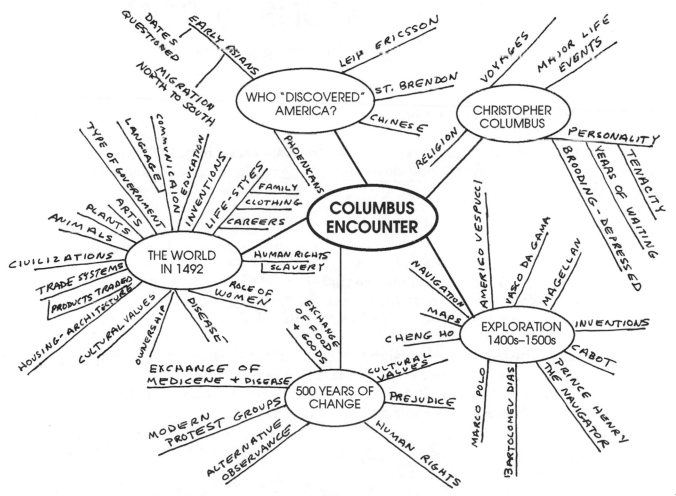

TIME LINE

Time lines are excellent aids to help students visualize time spans and sequences of events. Students will have more involvement in the time line and a greater sense of their own discovery of information if they brainstorm filling in a blank time line.

To make a world history time line, take six sheets of continuous-feed computer paper and lay out the whole sheet sideways. Using a yardstick and black marker, draw a line, one inch from the top, from one end of the paper to the other. Mark each inch with a vertical line. Your scale is 1" = 100 years. Begin with 4000 B.C. and end with A.D. 2000. At 500-year intervals, write in the year. Place a cross at the point where B.C. becomes A.D.

To make an age of exploration (1100–1600) time line, follow the above, except use a scale of 3" = 50 years. Begin with A.D. 1000 and end with A.D. 1600. Mark and write in the year every 50 years.

TEACHER DEMONSTRATION
How a Globe Becomes a Map

How do you make a round ball flat?

You will need a globe, an orange, paper towels, Peters' map (distributed by UNICEF), and a typical pull-down map of the world (most are Mercator maps).

Have students look at a globe while you ask the following:

- ◆ Count the oceans. How many are there?
- ◆ How many continents are there?
- ◆ What and where is the equator?
- ◆ Where is the North Pole? the South Pole?

Next, take the class on an imaginary trip. Explain that you need a map to know where to go. It is not possible to carry a large, round globe. You will need something thin and flat that you can fold. So how do you make something round like a ball become flat like a pancake?

DEMONSTRATION

1. Take an orange and pretend it is our planet Earth.
2. Show students that most maps are cut down the Pacific Ocean to avoid dividing land masses.
3. Don't cut all around the orange, only down one half.
4. Carefully, slide your fingers under the peel and gently pull the skin off the orange so it is in one spherical piece. This does work! Showing students the whole round peel is worth a thousand words.
5. To make the peel flat, open it at your cut, gently set it down on paper towels, inside skin down. Firmly press down on it with the palm of your hand until it is flat. The peel will tear; this is supposed to happen.
6. Have students look at the flattened peel and note all the spaces where they can see paper toweling where the peel is split. This is why distortion occurs on a flat map.
7. Explain that this distortion makes areas near the north and south poles seem much larger in relationship to other areas than they actually are.

MAP DISTORTION

Ask students to compare the Peters' map of the world, an old Mercator map of the world, and a globe. The globe and the Peters' map will show the continents and countries in the correct proportionate sizes. The Mercator (common) map shows Europe and the Northern Hemisphere larger than their relative size. Mr. Mercator made the basic map in Germany in 1538 and it became the accepted standard. Needless to say, this has added to most people's misunderstanding of the size of continents. The Peters' map is still not a perfect map and has its own distortion, but it is not as distorted as the Mercator map. Comparing the globe and two maps: What size is Greenland? South America?

What else do you see that is different? A globe represents the geography of the Earth better than a flat map. Which map is more like the globe?

THE COLUMBUS ENCOUNTER
A Multicultural View

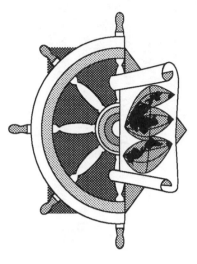

UNIT I

Part A: Who "Discovered" America? (Activities 1–4)

Part B: About Columbus (Activities 5–8)

Part C: The World in 1492 (Activities 9–14)

Part D: Explorations of the 1400s and 1500s (Activities 15 & 16)

Part E: 500 Years of Change (Activity 17)

Name _____

Date _____

The Columbus Encounter © 1992 Zephyr Press, Tucson, AZ

Part A: Who "Discovered" America?

1. SETTING THE STAGE

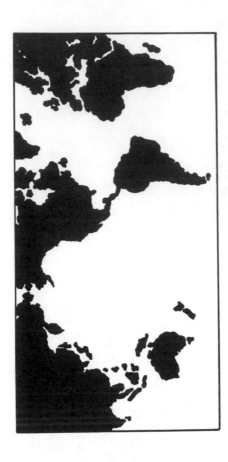

Find some books about:

Renaissance Europe
Christopher Columbus
The Aztecs and the Incas
Native North Americans before
  and after Columbus arrived
Ancient China
Africa in the 1400s and 1500s
Explorers

Think about a time long ago when there were no cars, trains, or airplanes. There were no engines to run machines. The people living in Europe, Africa, and Asia at that time did not know there were two more continents—North America and South America. The people in North and South America did not know about the people in Europe, Asia, and Africa. Make some guesses about what could happen if these two worlds came to learn about each other.

2. ACROSS THE LAND BRIDGE, ACROSS THE SEA

Thousands of years ago people lived in North and South America. Many experts believe that they came across a land bridge that used to exist between Asia and North America. These traveling nomads were probably following herds of wild animals, which they killed for food. Other experts think that some of these early peoples may have come from Africa or other places by boat and settled on the coasts of the Americas.

◆ With a group of your friends, make a diorama of a group of early people and some of the animals that lived 20,000 to 40,000 years ago. Use clay to make your figures, and paint or draw a background. It was very cold, so people probably wore clothes made of animal skins. To get ideas for your diorama, find some books that have pictures of early peoples in the Americas.

3. MYSTERIOUS VISITORS

Find some books that have pictures of very old items that have been found in North and South America. Then find pictures of similar objects that were found in places far away from America. It is possible that people from these faraway places crossed the oceans by boat and arrived in the Americas long before Columbus came.

◆ Draw pictures of 3 or 4 of the items found in the Americas that are like objects found far away. In what parts of the world were the objects found?

Part A: Who "Discovered" America?

4. LEIF THE LUCKY

Besides those who crossed the land bridge into America, Leif Ericsson, a Viking from Norway, and his crew are the only other people proven to have sailed to and lived in North America before Columbus's landing.

The main way we know that Leif landed in America is by the discovery of ruins of homes and tools left behind in the area where many stories say that Leif and his friends built a settlement.

◆ Find out about the adventures of Leif Ericsson. Then pretend that you are Leif or his sister, Freydis, who also settled in North America. You have taken a trip back to Iceland to see your friends and family and you are telling them what life is like in North America. Use a tape recorder to tape your story. Be sure to include what you see, what you eat, how you feel living there, and how it feels to be back home again.

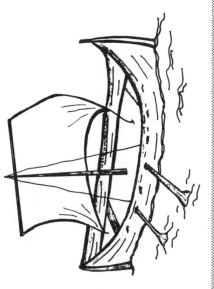

PART B: ABOUT COLUMBUS

Although Columbus is a very famous man, there are many questions about his life. This is because much written information about him was lost or was inaccurate. The following is based on what many many historians think is true.

Christopher Columbus was born about 500 years ago in Genoa, Italy. As a boy, Columbus probably sat on the docks of Genoa watching the ships and sailors come and go. Ships regularly unloaded spices, silks, gold, and treasures. About 1466, when Columbus was fifteen years old, he began working aboard ships in the Mediterranean Sea. Columbus's dream was to become very rich.

When he became a young man, Columbus sailed on ships that stayed near the coasts of Europe, Africa, England, Norway, and Iceland. He may have heard the stories of Leif Ericsson's voyages to North America 500 years earlier. He also studied maps and charts of early explorers and talked to sailors about where they had been.

In 1486, when Columbus was in his thirties, he began asking for money to hire men, build ships, and buy supplies to sail west to find the riches of the Indies and China. After being turned down by other kings, Columbus turned to King Ferdinand and Queen Isabella of Spain. Columbus had to wait for about eight years before they gave him the money he needed.

Many people today think that Columbus wanted to sail west to the Indies to prove that the Earth was round. This is not true. Educated people of the times knew the Earth was round; they just didn't know how big it was. Columbus insisted that the Earth was much smaller than most experts believed. Of course, Columbus was wrong. If the Americas had not been in the way, Columbus and his crew would have starved long before they reached the Indies.

Columbus's first voyage began on August 3, 1492, from Spain. Columbus was a very good navigator. After thirty-three days at sea, land was sighted during the night. When dawn came the crew landed on what most historians think is the island of San Salvador near Florida. Columbus and some of his men went ashore with banners. Even though he could clearly see that people already lived there, Columbus claimed the land for the Spanish king and queen.

The Columbus Encounter © 1992 Zephyr Press, Tucson, AZ

PART B: ABOUT COLUMBUS (continued)

The first exchanges with the Native Americans (a tribe called the Taino) were very friendly. Since Columbus thought he had reached the Indies, he called all the people he met "Indians." The gentle and curious people cooperated with Columbus and his men by helping them bring items ashore and finding food for them. When he was ready to move on, Columbus forced some of the Taino to go with him to act as his guides and interpreters. As Columbus traveled from island to island looking for gold and riches, he met different groups of Native Americans and found that each tribe had its own customs.

When he finally headed back to Spain, he forced several Native Americans to return with him. The king and queen were disappointed that Columbus had not found more gold or spices. However, they were fascinated by the people, plants, and animals that he brought back and they did bestow upon him the title of Admiral of the Ocean Sea and paid him some extra money.

On Columbus's second voyage he was in the Caribbean Sea for almost three years. He didn't find any great treasures and he faced problems with Spanish settlers, who quarreled and fought with each other, and with the Native Americans, who began to fight back when the Spaniards tried to take things from them. Columbus began taking Native Americans into slavery to ship back to Europe to sell. He thought maybe the king and queen could get rich this way. Columbus and his men were very mean to some of the Native Americans.

On Columbus's third voyage he was sent back to Spain in chains because he was not a good leader of a small town that he was in charge of. He was kept a prisoner on the ship. But the queen gave Columbus another chance, and on his fourth voyage he spent three more years sailing around the Caribbean and the eastern coast of Central America. He ended up marooned on an island. Native Americans supplied Columbus and his men with food for an entire year before help came.

Columbus died in Spain in 1506. He had opened the way to the Americas. He had started changes that made both the Americas and the rest of the world different forever.

Part B: About Columbus

5. THE FOUR VOYAGES OF CHRISTOPHER COLUMBUS

Sunday, 9 September 1492.

"This day we completely lost sight of land. Many men sighed and wept for fear they would not see it again for a long time." —C. Columbus

Columbus made four trips from Spain to the islands of the Caribbean and the northern edge of South America. His first trip was in 1492, and he came home from his last trip about twelve years later.

◆ Trace a world map. Then, using a different color for each trip, draw Columbus's four routes.

6. WHAT IS THE TRUTH?

Monday, 10 September 1492.

"Today I made one hundred eighty miles. I recorded only one hundred forty-four miles in order not to alarm the sailors." —C. Columbus

Read any version of *The Three Little Pigs*. Next read *The True Story of the Three Little Pigs* by A. Wolf as told to John Sciezka. Whom do you believe? Act out your version of the truth for your classmates.

Now read the biography provided in this book and/or read one of these biographies of Christopher Columbus: *Columbus Day* by Vicki Liestman or *First Biography: Christopher Columbus, Great Explorer* by David Adler.

Ask your school librarian to help you find a biography of Columbus that was written before 1985. Compare it with what you have just read. What is different? Does the older version talk about what life was like for Native Americans? What information about Columbus does it leave out? If you did not know this information, how would your view of what happened be different?

7. BIG OR SMALL?

Columbus's ships, the *Nina*, the *Pinta*, and the *Santa Maria*, were tiny compared to today's vessels. Historians and scientists estimate their size based on what cargo they were able to carry. The *Nina* carried twenty-two men, food, water, and supplies.

♦ Take a tape measure outside or into a hallway or large room. Measure an area the size of the *Nina*. Find out how many of your classmates could fit into your measured space.

♦ Draw a picture or make a diorama that shows what life might have been like on the *Nina*.

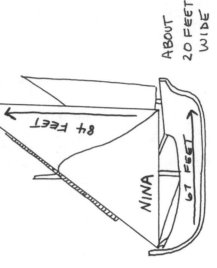

ABOUT 20 FEET WIDE

84 FEET

67 FEET

NINA

NINA

8. LET'S GO SAILING AND MEET ANOTHER WORLD

Compare the life-style of Columbus's crew on the *Santa Maria* with the life-style of the Native Americans. Find two areas in your room that you could use to display a variety of items: one area for the Americas before Columbus arrived and one area for Columbus's crew.

◆ In the first area hang a hammock, and make some tall paper trees. Put some brightly colored paper parrots in your trees. Use boxes or other items to make the kinds of houses that Native Americans lived in. Put sea shells on your beach, and make some special feather ornaments. Gather jewelry, corn, popcorn, beads, and other items.

◆ Then gather items that might be found on the *Santa Maria*, such as a compass, maps, charts of stars, an hourglass, ship's bell, flute, food, scrub brush, and a ship's log.

◆ Have some of your classmates be sailors and some be Native Americans. You do not understand each others' languages. You must make up your own sign language. After meeting, exchange some of your items, and tell how you might use these items from another culture.

9. THE AMERICAS: MANY MILLIONS STRONG

For many years it was thought that in 1492 there were about 10 million Native Americans in North and South America. However, scientists have studied ancient ruins and graves that show there may have been between 50 and 100 million. These people were divided into many groups or civilizations and had their own languages, customs, and religions. Three of these were the Incas, the Aztecs, and the Mound Builders.

◆ Find out where these civilizations lived. Draw or trace a map of the Americas and color in these civilizations using a different color for each.

◆ Then draw a picture or make a diorama of a building from one of these groups. Are there any buildings near where you live that look something like these buildings? If so, what kind of buildings are they?

The Columbus Encounter © 1992 Zephyr Press, Tucson, AZ

10. RENAISSANCE EUROPE: THE IMPORTANCE OF THE PRINTING PRESS

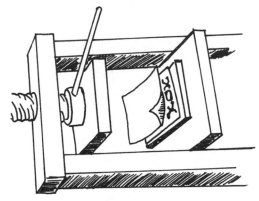

Before the Renaissance, many people in Europe were very poor and had difficult lives. During the Renaissance, which took place over several hundred years, many new ideas were developed that helped improve people's lives. One of these ideas was the *movable type printing press.* Before the printing press, books were written by hand. This took so long that only a few very rich people owned books.

◆ List five ways that your life would be different if you had no books.
Tell how you might learn facts and ideas if you had no books.

◆ Tell how your life would be different if we had no TVs.

11. THE ORIENT

Marco Polo was an Italian merchant who traveled in 1275 from Italy to China, where he saw such sights as firecrackers and paper that was used as money. Later, his travels were written about in *A Description of the World*, better known as *The Travels of Marco Polo*.

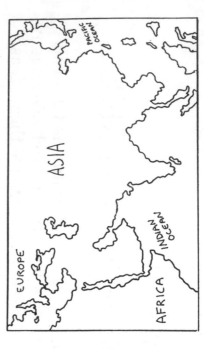

◆ Find out about Marco Polo. Draw or trace a map of the area where he traveled, and show where he visited.

◆ Then draw pictures or write descriptions of three or four of the things he saw that were not known in Italy at that time.

◆ Pretend that you are traveling with Marco Polo. Write a letter back home to a friend or your family describing the new things that you saw in China and at the court of Kublai Khan.

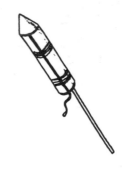

The Columbus Encounter © 1992 Zephyr Press, Tucson, AZ

12. THE ORIENT: SPICE OF LIFE

In 1492, spices were worth more than gold. People did not have refrigerators to keep their meat fresh. Instead, they used spices to preserve it and make older meat taste better. Spices did not grow in the cold climate of Europe. They grew on islands in what is now the country of Indonesia. Arab traders brought these spices to Europe and charged a very high price for them. Europeans hoped to get these spices more easily by sailing around Africa.

♦ Locate Indonesia on a map or globe. Find the Molucca Islands. What spices grow here? Use an encyclopedia or other book to find out what kinds of plants the spices grow on. What part of the plant are they?

OR

♦ Pretend you are an Arab merchant trying to sell spices. Make a picture poster to advertise your wares.

NUTMEG

CLOVES

13. AFRICA: ON THE MAP

Five major kingdoms were in Africa at the time that Columbus sailed for America. They were Songhai, Kongo, Benin, Luba, and Mwanamutapa.

◆ Draw or trace a map and locate these kingdoms. Color in their locations and color code your map legend to match. Use an atlas to find the names of countries that exist in these areas today. Draw in their outlines on your map and label them.

◆ Then shade in:

the Sahara Desert

the Kalahari Desert

the rain forest area

the Great Rift Valley

AFRICA

14. AFRICA: MANY TRADING KINGDOMS

Large cities with wide streets were busy centers of trade in Africa in 1492. Trade routes crossed Africa's interior. Arab ships sailed her coasts. Africans had developed the skills for making fine pieces of metal work and sculptures of wood, clay, and ivory.

◆ Read *Mufaro's Beautiful Daughter*, an African tale, by John Steptoe. Draw a picture of the city where the Great King lived. Be sure to put in some plants and animals you might find there.

OR

◆ In 1492 some people in Africa lived in villages. Houses with walls made of mud and roofs of straw were built in groups, with pasture and farmland surrounding them. Read *The Village of Round and Square Houses* by Ann Grifalconi. Draw a picture or make a model of this African village.

Part D: Explorations of the 1400s and 1500s

15. EXPLORERS' SEA ROUTES

Many explorers made long and dangerous trips during Columbus's times.

◆ Find out about Bartolomeu Dias. Draw a map showing where he sailed.

    OR

◆ Find out about Amerigo Vespucci. Tell where he sailed and what he is known for.

    OR

◆ Find out about Ferdinand Magellan. Where did he sail? Draw a picture of one of his adventures.

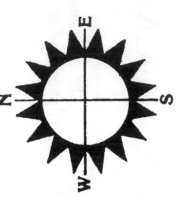

16. TROUBLE AT SEA

"The wind increased last night and the waves were frightful."
—C. Columbus

In 1492, when Columbus was in trouble in a storm, he had no way to communicate with anyone on land. When he was returning to Spain on his first journey, his ship was in such a bad storm that he thought it would sink and he and his crew would die. Columbus was afraid that no one in Europe would know that he had found what he thought was the Indies. So he quickly wrote about his trip on some paper and sealed it in a barrel. Then he threw the barrel overboard, hoping that if the ship sank, someone would find the message. Eventually the storm settled down and Columbus and his crew did make it back to Spain. No one ever found the message.

◆ Pretend that you found the barrel with Columbus's message about his trip. Write down what you think the message said.

17. A GIFT FOR YOU, A GIFT FOR ME

Before Columbus's first voyage, the Americas had no contact with Europe, Africa, and Asia. Some plants and animals in one area were not found in the other. Some foods, such as potatoes, tomatoes, and chili peppers, found only in the Americas, were developed by Native American farmers into plants that tasted good and were easy to grow.

◆ Find four other foods that grew only in the Americas before Columbus arrived. Draw pictures of them.

◆ Read the book *All Pigs on Deck* by Laura Fischetto. Pretend you are a Native American watching Columbus unload his ship. What difficulties is he having? How do you feel watching him? What does he need to learn?

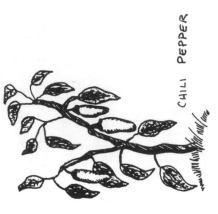

CHILI PEPPER

THE COLUMBUS ENCOUNTER

A Multicultural View

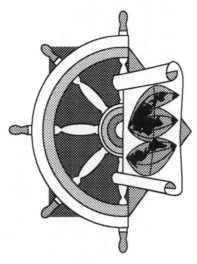

Part A: Who "Discovered" America? (Activities 1 & 2)

Part B About Columbus (Activities 3–7)

Part C: The World in 1492 (Activities 8–19)

Part D: Explorations of the 1400s and 1500s (Activities 20–22)

Part E: 500 Years of Change (Activities 23–28)

Name _____

Date _____

UNIT II

The Columbus Encounter © 1992 Zephyr Press, Tucson, AZ

Part A: Who "Discovered" America?

1. SETTING THE STAGE

By now you have probably read or heard that Columbus did not actually "discover" America. Before he landed in the Caribbean in 1492, there were many millions of people living in North and South America. According to most historians, these were the descendants of people from Asia who crossed the land bridge that once existed between Asia and Alaska. Others may have traveled by boat from Africa and settled in the Americas. Some people do not believe either of these theories about how the early peoples arrived on this continent.

◆ Study the different theories about how the first people came to the Americas. Which ideas seem most likely to you and why? Support your opinion with reasoning and/or evidence.

OR

◆ Pretend you were one of the first people to come to this continent. Write a play or short story about your adventures.

Part A: Who "Discovered" America?

2. EARLY ADVENTURERS

Besides the ancestors of Native Americans, Leif Ericsson, a Viking from Norway, and his crew are the only other people proven to have landed and lived in North America before Columbus.

◆ Find out about Leif's voyages and retell the stories about his trips into a tape recorder. Explain "oral tradition."

OR

◆ Many anthropologists think that other people may have come to the Americas before Columbus. Choose one of the following who might have made the journey and write a speech supporting your beliefs: St. Brendon (an Irish Monk), the Phoenicians, other Vikings, the Welsh Prince, or the Chinese monk Huishen.

OR

◆ Find out about the Sioux, Iroquois, Navajo, or Yaqui creation legends. Draw a picture or make a diorama showing their beliefs.

OR

◆ Tell about Thor Heyerdahl's expeditions and what his voyages proved.

PART B: ABOUT COLUMBUS

One would think there would be a wealth of documented information about a man as well known as Christopher Columbus. However, what we know about the famous explorer is based on a few documents that have survived.

Columbus himself wrote a log or diary of his first voyage, telling many details about the trip. The original log was given to the king and queen of Spain, who had a copy made. Eventually both the original and the copy were lost. Fortunately Bartolomé de las Casas, a Catholic priest, had access to the first copy and made another copy. Although he did edit and summarize some, and he did not understand all the navigating terms, his copy is considered to be reliable.

After he returned, Columbus also wrote a letter summarizing his trip. He reported that he had found the spice islands of the Indies, causing many people to conclude that the treasures of China must be nearby. Due to the use of the printing press, the letter was easily copied and distributed throughout Europe, encouraging many to sail west across the Atlantic.

Secondary sources include the diaries of de las Casas, who lived in the Americas for forty-five years and wrote prolifically as a defender of Native American rights, and those of Diego, Columbus's son, who became his father's biographer. Other sources include diaries of men on ships with Columbus, church records, and government documents. Even though many facts are still disputed, what follows is information that many recent historians accept as true.

Columbus's Times (1451–1506)

Columbus's lifetime spanned the end of the Middle Ages and the beginning of the Renaissance. The Middle Ages were characterized by ignorance, intolerance, starvation, and misery. Columbus lived much of his life in Spain, under the terrifying brutality of the Spanish Inquisition. The Middle Ages gradually gave way to the Renaissance, a more intellectually enlightened time of educated and tolerant outlooks and new interest in the arts and sciences.

The Columbus Encounter © 1992 Zephyr Press, Tucson, AZ

PART B: ABOUT COLUMBUS (continued)

Columbus's Childhood (1451–1465)

Although there are no records of Columbus's birth, some documents lead historians to believe that he was probably born in 1451 in Genoa, Italy. Historians believe that Columbus was brought up in a middle-class working family. His father, Domenico, was a tavern keeper and proprietor of a weaver's shop. His mother was Susanna Fontanarossa, and as far as historians know, Columbus had three brothers and one sister. As a child, he did not learn to read or write. Although his native tongue was Italian, Columbus learned to read and write Spanish when he was an adult.

Genoa was one of the great ports of the time and ships regularly unloaded spices, silks, gold, and other exotic treasures. Columbus's interest in the sea came naturally, as it did for most young boys who sat on the docks watching the ships and sailors come and go. The printed account of Marco Polo's trips added fuel to Columbus's developing dream of a life on the sea. He did not dream of being a famous explorer or an altruistic anthropologist studying other cultures. Rather, his dream was to become incredibly rich. Later, when he began formulating the idea of traveling west to the Indies, he added the desire of converting native peoples to Christianity.

Marco Polo's book was part fact and part fantasy, but his stories added to the European view that riches were to be easily plucked from the Orient, if only a merchant could figure out a safer way to get there. The land routes presented danger from thieves, deadly deserts, towering mountains, and competition from traders from other countries. Also, it took a year to get to the Orient by land.

Columbus, the Young Man (1466–1475)

Around 1466, when Columbus was fifteen years old, he probably began working aboard ships that sailed trade routes on the Mediterranean Sea. Later he traveled these routes as a wool merchant, buying, selling, and trading woolen cloth. Eventually, Columbus left the Mediterranean and sailed the Atlantic, keeping mainly to the coasts of Europe and Africa.

The Columbus Encounter © 1992 Zephyr Press, Tucson, AZ

PART B: ABOUT COLUMBUS (continued)

At one point he was on a ship in battle off the coast of Portugal. The ship sank, but he clung to a piece of wood and made it to shore. Some local people helped him, and he spent some time recovering in Portugal. Though Columbus's stay was not long, he was introduced to the Portuguese enthusiasm for discovery. Later he came back to glean information at the Center for Discovery, which had been established by Prince Henry the Navigator. Here sailors, map makers, adventurers, and dreamers met to share information on the possibilities of the sea. Without this sharing of ideas, many discoveries probably would have been delayed.

During the next few years, Columbus went on voyages to Africa, England, Norway, and Iceland, where he undoubtedly heard the stories of Leif Ericsson's voyages and settlement in America almost 500 years earlier in 1014.

In 1486 Columbus began his years of requesting money for men, ships, and supplies to sail west to find the riches of the Indies. When the king of Portugal refused his request, Columbus turned to Queen Isabella of Castile and King Ferdinand of Aragon. However, because Spain was still involved in war, the government was using all its money to pay for war supplies.

The Waiting Years (1486–1492)

After Columbus had petitioned them several times, the king and queen of Spain finally formed a committee of experts to study Columbus's proposal. Today many people think that part of Columbus's proposal was to prove that the Earth was round. However, educated people of the time knew the Earth was round; they just didn't know how big it was. Columbus insisted that the Earth was much smaller than most people believed. The committee concluded that Columbus's estimate was incorrect. (The committee proved to be correct; had the Americas not been in the way, Columbus and his crew would have starved long before they reached Cipango [Japan], which is where the explorer thought he would make his first landing.)

Finally, after Columbus had waited for seven years in frustration and despair, the queen and king unexpectedly granted permission for the voyage. Spain's wars were over and they had enough money to support Columbus's venture. Their own dreams of personal wealth, as well as

The Columbus Encounter © 1992 Zephyr Press, Tucson, AZ

PART B: ABOUT COLUMBUS (continued)

hope of enough gold to support an army large enough to recapture Jerusalem from the Moors, prompted the sovereigns to take a chance on Columbus's idea.

The Four Voyages (1492–1504)

Columbus's first voyage began on August 3, 1492, from Palos, Spain. The crew put their faith in God and in Columbus's resolute insistence that he knew where he was going. At home with the sea, Columbus was a master navigator gifted with an instinct for "dead reckoning," an imprecise method of setting a ship on course.

On October 12, after 33 days at sea, land was sighted during the night by a crew member. When dawn came, the crew landed on what most historians think is the island of San Salvador. According to Columbus's log, the crew observed "naked people, very green trees, many waters, and fruits of different kinds." Columbus and some of his men went ashore with banners representing King Ferdinand and Queen Isabella. Even though he could clearly see the land was already inhabited, Columbus claimed it for Spain.

The first exchanges with the Native Americans were very friendly. The curious Taino cooperated with Columbus and his men by helping them bring items ashore and helping them find food. (The Native Americans were called Taino [or Arawak], but Columbus called all the people he came across "Indians" because he thought he had landed in the Indies.) Later, as Columbus traveled from island to island, he met different groups of Native Americans and found that while some groups or tribes had similar customs, others were very different from each other. Three months later, just before Columbus headed for Spain, he met the first armed Native Americans he had seen on the trip. After a short skirmish, Columbus's men subdued the small band.

Before that point, Columbus had taken whatever he wanted because the Native Americans were not armed and offered little resistance. He had forced some of the first group he met to go with him on his ship to act as his guides and interpreters. When he finally headed back to Spain, he forced several Native Americans to return with him, leaving thirty-nine of his men on the island of Hispaniola to set up a camp in a place he called Villa de la Navidad (Christmas Town).

The Columbus Encounter © 1992 Zephyr Press, Tucson, AZ

PART B: ABOUT COLUMBUS (continued)

When Columbus arrived in Spain he received a hero's welcome, although the king and queen were disappointed that he did not bring back more riches. They did bestow upon him the title of Admiral of the Ocean Sea and met the other financial demands that Columbus had negotiated.

On Columbus's second voyage, he remained in the Caribbean for almost three years. Things did not go well on this visit. He could not find the rivers of gold he had promised Ferdinand and Isabella. He faced problems with rebellious Spanish settlers. The Native Americans were not as passive as they had been at first; they began to fight back to avoid being forced into slavery.

On Columbus's third voyage, he landed on the coast of South America. It was so beautiful, he thought he had found the Garden of Eden. This voyage ended in shame. Columbus was sent back to Spain in chains for his inability to govern a permanent European settlement called Santo Domingo. The captain of the return ship offered to take off the chains, but Columbus refused. When the queen sent for Columbus, she had his chains removed, and he was given the chance to make one more voyage.

On his fourth and final voyage, he spent three more years sailing around the Caribbean and the east coast of Central America looking for China. He never accepted the fact that he was not anywhere near China, although some other explorers already concluded this. He had more bad luck on this trip and ended up marooned on an island for a year before help came. This time Columbus forced his crew members to stay aboard the ship, which had run aground on the beach. He knew he would be dependent on the Native Americans to supply his crew with food, and he didn't want the sailors stealing from or mistreating the tribe. Reluctantly, the Native Americans did supply them with food for an entire year.

Columbus's Legacy

Columbus died in Spain in 1506, not long after he arrived home from his fourth voyage. Though he died in relative obscurity and never knew he had not reached the Orient, he had opened the floodgates to the Americas. As a result, treasure seekers and soul savers had begun a chain of events that totally changed both the Americas and the rest of the world forever.

The Columbus Encounter © 1992 Zephyr Press, Tucson, AZ

3.   COLUMBUS: HOW DO WE KNOW WHAT WE KNOW?

"Men occasionally stumble over the truth, but most of them pick themselves up and hurry away as if nothing happened." —Winston Churchill

Read the biography provided with this book and read about Columbus from other books in your classroom or library. Be sure to read at least TWO accounts of his life. How are the two accounts different?

> *THEN . . . .*

◆ Find out what is meant by primary sources, secondary sources, hearsay, and speculation. What are the primary sources (if any) that tell historians about Christopher Columbus's first voyage? his fourth voyage?

> OR

◆ In an essay, tell what historians mean when they say . . .

"it would seem . . . ."

"it is probable . . . ."

"we can deduce . . . ."

4. THE WORLD IS ROUND

One of the myths about Columbus is that he was a man obsessed with proving that the world was round. Educated people, including Columbus, already knew this.

- ◆ Find out who Ptolemy was and explain what he thought about the shape and size of the world. Why did Columbus think the world was much smaller than the scholars of his time thought it was?

> OR

- ◆ What explorer is given credit for finally proving that the world is round? What happened to him before his ship returned home?

5. ON BOARD THE SANTA MARIA

Imagine you are a cabin boy on the *Santa Maria* during Columbus's first voyage to the Americas. What might be some reasons you would want to sail with Columbus? (Remember that no one knew much about him on his first voyage.)

◆ In a diorama, a drawing, or a play show what your day is like. For example, where do you sleep? What do you eat? What do you do for fun? for work? What is the ocean like?

OR

◆ In a diorama, a drawing, or a play show what happens when you land in America. For example, what do you see? Do you go back to Spain with Christopher Columbus? What happens to you?

THEN . . . .

◆ Tell how your trip changes your life and the way you look at things.

Part B: About Columbus

6. KEEPING A LOG OR JOURNAL

Monday, 10 September 1492.

"Today I made one hundred eighty miles. I recorded only one hundred forty-four miles in order not to alarm the sailors." —C. Columbus

For one week keep two journals of where you go and what happens in your life each day. In the first journal, write whatever you want, including your feelings. This journal will be confidential—no one will read it but you. The second journal will be open to the public. Your parents, teachers, friends, enemies, etc., will be able to read everything you write if they want to.

At the end of the week, compare the two journals and answer these questions:

◆ In which journal were you most honest about your feelings?

◆ In the second journal did you alter or leave out anything because you thought others might not approve or because it was too complicated to write about or you got tired of writing?

◆ What other differences did you notice about your journals?

◆ Whom do you think Christopher Columbus kept his log for?

◆ Why would it have been important for Columbus's log to be acceptable to the king and queen?

◆ What does the term "public relations" mean? In what ways was Columbus a good "PR" man? In what ways wasn't he?

7. WHAT IF . . .

"You have not converted a man because you have silenced him." —C. Morley

Countries have taken over other countries by force for thousands of years, and it is still happening today. However, many countries, political leaders, and everyday citizens are trying to solve conflicts without war.

◆ How would you feel if armed representatives of another country came and planted a flag of their country in your front yard and then came into your house without knocking and ate your food without asking?

◆ What methods could you encourage your parents/neighbors to take to solve the problem without violence? Who might you call for help? What laws protect your rights? What laws protect the representatives' rights?

Part C: The World in 1492

8. WHAT WAS LIFE LIKE IN 1492?

♦ Find out what the average daily life was like in 1492. Draw two pictures or make dioramas showing the kinds of food, clothing, and shelter that Europeans and Native Americans had in the late 1400s. What luxuries did each world have? What did they use for trade?

   OR

♦ Find out who was "in charge" of the following countries in the late 1400s and what type of government each country had: Spain (or the area we now call Spain), Italy, Portugal, France, England, the Caribbean, the African nation of New Guinea, China, and two areas in North or South America.

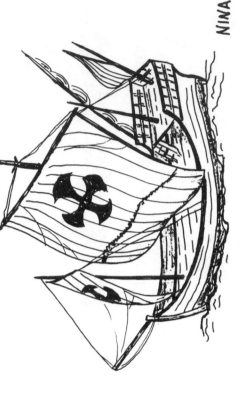

NINA

Part C: The World in 1492

9. SLAVERY

"No man is good enough to govern another man without his consent."
—Abraham Lincoln

During much of history, groups of people have considered it their right to be masters over other groups of people.

During the 1400s, where were there

◆ white slaves and who were their masters?

◆ black slaves and who were their masters?

◆ Native North American slaves and who were their masters?

◆ Native South American slaves and who were their masters?

◆ Chinese slaves and who were their masters?

Often in history, slavery was not a racial issue. On what basis did the "masters" think they had a right to rule the slaves?

What is the attitude toward slavery in most of the world today?

10. THE CRUSADES AND THE SPANISH INQUISITION

◆ The Crusades

Find out why the Crusades were fought. Describe the Crusades, the years they covered, and where the battles were fought. What kinds of weapons were used? What kind of medical care was available to the wounded? Who "won" the Crusades? What benefit did the Crusades have in modernizing Europe?

OR

◆ The Spanish Inquisition

Find out who the victims of the Spanish Inquisition were. How long did the Inquisition last? How were Queen Isabella and King Ferdinand involved in the Inquisition?

11. RELIGIOUS WARS TODAY

◆ Where are there "religious wars" going on in the world today? What methods are used to try to solve conflicts between groups or nations today? Give three examples of methods that you think would work for solving conflicts.

OR

◆ When the American Constitution was being drawn up, one of the main issues for the new country was *separation of church and state*. Considering what you have learned about Europe from 1400 to 1700, why do you think European settlers would want to separate religious issues from government issues?

OR

◆ Name three countries that have separation of church and state today and three countries that do not. What do you think are some of the advantages and disadvantages of each system?

12. THE ORIENT: LAND OF TREASURES

The Silk Road was the trade route used by Europeans and Chinese merchants to trade their goods. Find out which countries the Silk Road crossed.

♦ Find out why Europeans wanted silk so much. Explain to a friend how the Chinese got silk and why they tried to keep it a secret.

OR

♦ The Orient was a source of great excitement to Europeans. They valued its many treasures. Today it may be hard to understand what Europeans thought was so wonderful about spices that we can buy cheaply in any grocery store. Find out why the Europeans valued spices more highly than gold. Explain to a friend what plants spices come from and what people of Columbus's time used them for.

NUTMEG

CLOVES

The Columbus Encounter © 1992 Zephyr Press, Tucson, AZ

Part C: The World in 1492

13. THE AMERICAS: MANY MILLIONS STRONG

Experts long believed that when Columbus first came to the Americas, about 10 million Native Americans inhabited the continents. However, recent archaeological studies of ancient cities and grave sites indicate the population may have been between 50 and 100 million. Continuing studies may provide a more exact figure.

These people were divided into many groups or civilizations and had different languages, customs, and religions. Six of these were the Incas, the Aztecs, the Mound Builders, the Taino, the Eskimos, and the Iroquois.

◆ Trace a map and show where each of these groups lived. Put each tribe name or a symbol for that tribe on the map.

14. NAMES

Many state names come from Native American words.

◆ Look up five of the states listed to find out what tribe the name comes from and what the word means: Alabama, Iowa, Nebraska, Connecticut, Alaska, Missouri, Wyoming, Ohio, Arkansas, Oklahoma, Illinois, Arizona.

◆ Does your city or a nearby town or county have a Native American name? If not, how about a park, lake, or river? Find out what the word means.

◆ Early Native Americans often gave their children descriptive names, like Running Deer or Yellow Hawk or Standing Bear. If you are Native American, do you have such a name? What is it? If you are not Native American or don't have a descriptive name, what special name would you like to have? Write it, then draw a picture of your name if you like.

15. BARTOLOMÉ DE LAS CASAS

"The only thing necessary for the triumph of evil is for good men to do nothing."
—Edmund Burke

Bartolomé de las Casas was a Spanish priest who went to the Caribbean islands a few years after Columbus's first landing.

Las Casas was a prolific writer who took it upon himself to write the history of the islands and of Central and South America. He lived and wrote in the area for 45 years. He was an outspoken critic of the brutal treatment the Native Americans received at the hands of Columbus, the Spanish, and other Europeans.

◆ Pretend that you are interviewing Father de las Casas. What 10 questions would you ask him and how do you think he might answer?

16. AFRICA: KINGDOMS AND TRADE CENTERS

In 1492, long before Europeans began to explore Africa's interior, many highly organized kingdoms and trade centers were in existence there. We are limited somewhat in our knowledge of these kingdoms and centers because the Africans had no writing system and therefore left no written record. Their artwork, especially in sculpture, metal working, and stone architecture, shows they were highly skilled artisans.

AFRICA

◆ Five major kingdoms in Africa in the late 1400s and early 1500s were Songhai, Kongo, Benin, Luba, and Mwanamutapa. Trace a map and locate these kingdoms. Color them on your map and color code your map legend to match. Use an atlas to find the names of modern countries that exist in these areas today. Draw in their outlines on your map and label them.

◆ Then shade in the Sahara Desert, the Kalahari Desert, the rain forest area, and the Great Rift Valley. Add them to your map legend.

17. AFRICA: VILLAGE LIFE

Community life based on close-knit small village groups was a strength in Africa. The family and village helped maintain law and order, harmony and balance.

◆ Using books on Africa, draw a picture or make a model of an African village. Show how the houses might be arranged. What were they made of?

OR

◆ Draw a picture or re-create a piece of African sculpture or metalwork.

18. RENAISSANCE EUROPE: FAMOUS ARTISTS

Renaissance is a word that means *rebirth*. It is used to describe a period of time in Europe when many new discoveries were made and new ideas were put forth. Two famous artists of this time were Michelangelo and Leonardo da Vinci (who was also an inventor).

◆ Choose one artist and look at some of his paintings. These artists' pictures are worth thousands of dollars today. Why are they valued so highly? Pick out two or three of your favorite paintings and study them for a long time. What do you especially like about the paintings? Why do you think people liked these paintings 500 years ago? Why do you think people still like them today? Talk these questions over with some classmates.

19. THE INFLUENCE OF THE PRINTING PRESS

The news of Columbus's first voyage raced through Europe—partly because of the invention of the movable type printing press.

◆ What was so important about this invention and how did it affect the world of learning? How did people learn new facts and ideas before they had the printing press? List five ways your life would be different without books.

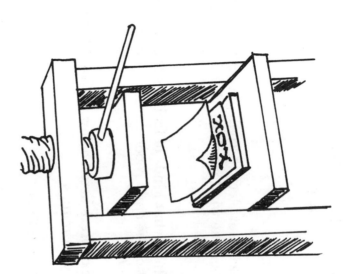

Part D: Explorations of the 1400s and 1500s

20. EXPLORERS

Explorers of the 1400s and 1500s used ships without electric, coal, gas, or nuclear power. Their ships were powered instead by the winds. When the wind was still, the ship did not move, except to drift with the ocean current.

◆ Define the following words and explain what kinds of feelings the sailors in 1492 might have when they heard them as part of the daily report: *dead calm, run with the wind, squall coming,* and *waterspout ahead.*

◆ On a map, draw in the trips of the explorers listed below. Use a different color for each man's trip and make a code key for your map.

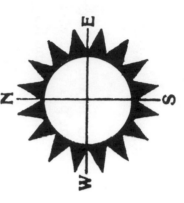

Vasco da Gama	Bartolomeu Dias
Amerigo Vespucci	Ferdinand Magellan
Hernando Cortés	Francisco Pizarro
Marco Polo	

◆ Who was Prince Henry the Navigator?

Part D: Explorations of the 1400s and 1500s

21. NAVIGATION

Sunday, 23 September, 1492.

"The crew is grumbling about the wind. The changing wind, along with the flat sea, has led the men to believe we will never get home." —C. Columbus

- Columbus could not have reached the Americas without technology and "know how" borrowed from China—the magnetic compass and the stern post rudder—and from Arabia—the lateen sail. Find out about these inventions in your encyclopedias (under "Inventions," "Ship," "Caravel," and "Sailing") and describe each of them. How did these inventions change European abilities to sail on long voyages far from land?

- Draw a picture or diagram of one invention.

  OR

- Write about Chinese boats and Chinese explorations of the world (by boat) before and during the 1500s.

  OR

- Write about Polynesian navigation and boats. What did Polynesian maps look like?

22. CROSSWORD PUZZLE

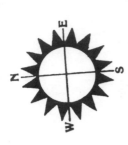

ACROSS

4. Viewpoint of Europeans or their descendants.
6. First island where Columbus started a settlement.
8. Amerigo _____.
11. Columbus's smallest ship (first voyage).
13. Instruments used by ocean navigators.
14. Queen _____ of Spain.
15. What Columbus believed he would find in the Indies.
16. Early Americans who built a great civilization.
18. "_____ reckoning."
20. _____ Ericson, Viking explorer.
21. Type of ships Columbus used on his four voyages.
24. A disease Europeans brought to the Americas.
25. Period of warring between Christians and others.
28. Columbus's flagship on his first voyage.
31. One of Columbus's ships.
32. The spice-growing countries of India and Asia.
33. A spice.
36. The capital of this country is Lisbon.
37. _____ Builders; early inhabitants of the Americas.
39. Marco _____.
40. _____ Henry, the Navigator.
41. An oversimplified picture of an entire group.
42. People who once ruled Mexico.

DOWN

1. King _____ of Spain.
2. Columbus wore these on his third voyage home.
3. An island in the Caribbean: _____ Republic.
5. Term for historians who write in realistic terms about heroes who have become legends.
7. The trade route from Europe to China.
9. A starchy food the Native Americans gave Europe.
10. Islands off Africa where Columbus stopped.
12. Explorer credited with circling the globe first.
17. Most of Columbus's sailors were of this nationality.
19. The Atlantic Ocean was called the Sea of _____.
22. Adventuresome Norse explorers.
23. The name for Japan during Columbus's times.
26. In 1492 there were about 500 tribes of _____ in North America.
27. The captain of the *Pinta* on Columbus's first voyage.
29. A period of "rebirth" following the Middle Ages.
30. Most explorers were not very _____. They were looking for wealth or fame.
34. Bartolomeu Dias rounded the Cape of _____.
35. A direction-finding instrument that always shows north.
38. To settle and take over lands for a distant government.

23. EVERYTHING'S DIFFERENT

Since Columbus stepped off his ship and onto a Caribbean island in 1492, many significant changes have taken place. Choose a country in North or South America. To show some of these changes, fill in the chart below.

	1492	1990s
Native population		
Population of African descent		
Type of religion(s)		
Number of cities with over 1 million people		
Types of transportation		
Recreational activities		
Women's roles		
Men's roles		
Schools/learning systems		
Wars		
Sources of power/energy		
Wildlife/Wilderness		
Political system(s)		

24. DEADLY DISEASE

After the arrival of Europeans in America, it wasn't swords or guns that killed many of the Native Americans. Instead, it was the diseases the Europeans brought. For example, the Native Americans had not built up any immunity to smallpox and typhoid.

Over three and one-half million people died in a smallpox epidemic in Mexico. Some historians believe that between 1519 and 1597 central Mexico's population fell from 11 million to 2 million due to disease.

A smallpox epidemic weakened the Inca civilization in Peru so severely that the Spaniards were able to conquer them easily. It is estimated that 90 percent of the Native American population in both North and South America died of disease soon after the arrival of the Europeans.

◆ Compare and contrast these epidemics with the arrival of the "Black Plague" in Europe in 1348.

25. NATIVE AMERICAN VOICES

Choose one of the following Native American issues to study. After you have learned about it, write a newspaper article expressing your opinion about the issue. Collect other students' articles and put together a newsletter about these issues.

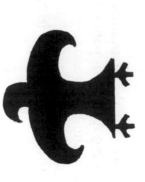

- ◆ Native land/water/mineral rights

- ◆ Museum/repatriation of bones/artifact issues

- ◆ Textbook distortion

- ◆ An issue that is important in your area

OR

- ◆ Choose one of the following Native Americans and, after reading about him or her, create a painting, a drawing, or a collage using symbols that represent that person's life.

Dennis Banks	Oscar Howe	Chief Seattle
Thomas Banyaca	Red Jacket	Virginia Driving Hawk Sneve
Ben Nighthorse Campbell	Wilma Mankiller	Jake Swamp
La Donna Harris	Maria Martinez	Floyd Westerman
Crazy Horse	Russell Means	

26. CHANGED FOREVER

When Europe became aware of the Americas the world of human beings was changed forever.

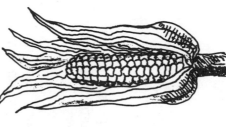

- ◆ List three positive and three negatives changes that occurred.

- ◆ List five items that Europe, Africa, or Asia gave to the Americas.

- ◆ List five items the Americas gave to Europe, Africa, or Asia that they didn't have before.

The Columbus Encounter © 1992 Zephyr Press, Tucson, AZ

27. CULTURAL STEREOTYPES

"The less secure a man is, the more likely he is to have extreme prejudice."
—Clint Eastwood

One of the definitions of *culture* is that it is all the things about a group of people that are similar. These similarities could include music, art, movies, religion or beliefs, family style, legends and heroes, work, language, holidays, and many other factors.

While people within a certain culture may have many things in common, they also develop as unique individuals. Sometimes people *outside* a certain culture get the impression that all people within a certain culture are exactly the same. This is called "cultural stereotyping."

◆ Give an example of cultural stereotyping. What might be harmful about cultural stereotyping to the people that *are part of* a specific culture? What might be harmful about cultural stereotyping to people *outside* a particular culture making a judgment about those of another culture?

◆ Think about the different kinds of cultural clashes that took place fifty years after Columbus came to the Caribbean. What kind of cultural classes exist today? What is the difference between culture and race?

28. WHY IS HISTORY SUBJECTIVE?

In your study of Columbus, you have seen that history can be interpreted subjectively.

◆ Define objective and subjective. Then write a summary of a book you have read, a TV show you have watched, a magazine article you have read, an incident on the playground, or a misunderstanding between you and a friend.

   Write your summary so that it is technically factual but not accurate in the overall impression that it gives to the reader or viewer. You might do this by omitting key facts or by changing a few words, so that the meaning changes.

   After you have altered your piece, read your interpretation to your group and then tell them what really happened.

   OR

◆ Describe what you think future historians will say about the twentieth century (1900–1999). (You might read *Motel of the Mysteries* by David Macaulay for inspiration.) Some issues might include violence, energy use, education, water use, forest and wildlife management, eating habits, men's and women's roles, business/industry, entertainment, computers, etc.

◆ If you could re-create a portion of history, what would you have happen? What can we do to shape and guide the legacy we leave to future generations?

EXPLORING THE ARTS

An opportunity to integrate art experiences within an academic content area

While each component—the Self-directed Learning Unit and Exploring the Arts—is a complete and valid learning experience in itself, together they provide a more comprehensive and lasting educational experience for the learner.

The Columbus Encounter © 1992 Zephyr Press, Tucson, AZ

A MOBILE: WORLD OF 1492

Find examples of artwork from the late 1400s by Native North Americans, Aztecs, Incas, Chinese, Indonesians, Arabs, Renaissance Europeans, and Africans—from the kingdoms of Benin, Mwanamutapa, Songhai, the Kongo, or the Luba. (Shirley Glubok's art books can be very helpful.)

◆ Make a mobile:

Fold a piece of construction paper in half twice, making quarters.

Draw four pictures representing the arts of different cultures, one in each section. If you want more than four pictures in your mobile, use a second piece of construction paper.

Color or paint your drawings. Then cut them out and color or paint the back sides.

Using a coat hanger and string or other materials, make a mobile with your pictures.

AFRICAN MASKS

In some African tribal ceremonies people put on masks and costumes to dance and act out stories. Tribespeople believe a person disguised in a mask can change into the spirit represented by the mask to tell young people the ways of their culture and tribe.

◆ Find some books on African art and study the designs and colors used in African masks. Make a rough sketch of a mask, then draw it on a piece of poster board. Cut it out, making holes for the eyes and mouth. Punch one hole on each side and tie a string to fit your head so you can wear your mask. Think of a story to tell while wearing your mask, and share it with your class or with a few friends.

The Columbus Encounter © 1992 Zephyr Press, Tucson, AZ

PRE-COLUMBIAN ART

Where does the term Pre-Columbian come from?

Ancient Peruvians had no writing system, so they left us no books to tell us how they lived. However, in the ruins of their buildings and graves, archaeologists have found many samples of their magnificent clay pottery. The pictures on the pots, either painted or etched, and the shape of the pottery show us what the men, women, and children looked like, what they wore, how they played and worked, what weapons and clothes their soldiers wore, and what gods they worshipped.

◆ Study photographs of this pottery, and then make your own clay figures. They could show what someone might have looked like during the time of the Incas, or they could show people of our time.

THE "PEOPLING" OF THE AMERICAS

The "peopling" of the Americas has, as you have learned, gone back for at least 25,000 years, perhaps even 40,000 years.

◆ Make a mural of the different people who have come to the Americas. You could begin with the Asian nomads who probably crossed over the land bridge in the ice ages. You might include scenes from such Native American cultures as the Inuit, the Cliff Dwellers (Anasazi), and the Maya. You might add the Viking settlement of Leif Ericsson, the Mound Builders, the buffalo hunters of the Great Plains, and the unproven voyages of St. Brenden, the Chinese, and other possible visitors to early America. Perhaps add the Aztecs, the Incas, Christopher Columbus, the Spaniards, the Pilgrims, black slaves from Africa, the Dutch, the Irish, the Italians, Greeks, Chinese, Vietnamese, and any ancestors from your own family who came to the Americas from another country.

How will you end your mural?

Who is here today?

What is in the future for us all?

A TIPI OF THE GREAT PLAINS

For centuries Native American buffalo hunters of the Great Plains used designs as symbols to decorate their belongings. One place they drew or painted these symbols was on the buffalo hides they used to make their tipis (or tepees). Many of the designs were geometric. Other designs were pictographs. Often the tipi owner included symbols based on dreams or painted a personal "totem" on the door flap. (A totem is an animal or other object from nature that is a specific family's or person's symbol.)

◆ Make a class tipi using a section made by each student. Cut a large section from a brown paper grocery bag. Shape it so it looks something like a buffalo hide. Paint or draw symbols on your hide.

Now take 5 or 6 strong pieces of rope and hang or tie them to the ceiling, all coming together at the top and circling out at the bottom like a tipi. Tape these sections of rope to the floor with clear plastic package tape.

Now you are ready to staple each student's "buffalo hide" to the tipi. Twenty-five or more hides will cover your tipi nicely.

◆ Read about the Native Americans of the Great Plains. What would they have put inside their tipis?

A CHINESE SCROLL

Many centuries ago the Chinese began painting on silk scrolls, which are long bands of silk that could be rolled up. Later, after the Chinese had invented paper (though still nearly 2,000 years ago), paper was used for scrolls.

A hanging scroll is a vertical (up-and-down) picture and is hung on the wall for others to admire. A hand scroll is a horizonal (side-to-side) picture that is unrolled little by little for others to see. Landscapes and animals are among the subjects painted on scrolls. Artists often stamped their seals or signatures on scrolls. Sometimes they even included a poem. Many famous Chinese paintings are done in black ink.

◆ To make your own scroll, use a long sheet of paper. Paint in black water color or black poster paints. Be sure you've included your seal or signature. Let your scroll dry completely. You may want to write in a poem now or go back over some of your drawing in black ink. Now roll up your scroll and tie it in a roll with a ribbon, or hang it on the wall.

The Columbus Encounter © 1992 Zephyr Press, Tucson, AZ

COLUMBUS'S SIGNATURE IN "CODE"

Columbus signed his name in an elaborate and unusual code. Part of his signature stood for the first letters of Latin words and the bottom line used two Latin words.

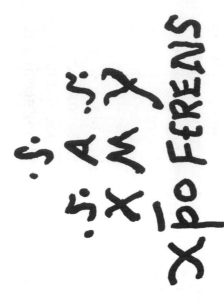

S - Servus
   (servant)

S - Supplex   A - Altisimi   S - Salvatoris
(Humble)   (on High)   (of the Savior)

X - Christus   M - Maria   Y - Yoseph
(Christ)   (Mary)   (Joseph)

Xpo Ferens - Christoferens
           (Christbearer)

All together, the initials and words stood for Humble Servant of the Savior on High, Christ, Mary, Joseph. The Christbearer.

◆ Write a line describing yourself in about 8 words. Use the first initials of the words you choose to design a special code signature.

The Columbus Encounter © 1992 Zephyr Press, Tucson, AZ

WORLD FAIR AND FEAST

One way to acknowledge the world of the Americas meeting the world of Europe, Africa, and Asia is with a World Fair and Feast. Display the work you have done. Set up eight main tables or display areas in your room, one table each for Europe, Africa, the Orient, the Americas, Columbus, Exploration and Discovery, the Renaissance, and 500 Years of Change.

At your celebration, you might:

◆ Display your reports, creative writing, drawings, crafts, models, artifacts, maps, mobiles.
◆ Set out books, pictures, charts.
◆ Play music from Peru, Indonesia, China, and Africa; Native American music or music from the Renaissance; sounds of the rain forest or sea.
◆ Make signs and banners to label each area.
◆ Make a collage of your topic.
◆ Perform a play, skit, interview, debate, song, or dance; read a poem you wrote; or read a famous quotation.
◆ Invite guests; make and send invitations.
◆ Station students to demonstrate and explain what you have done.

For the feast:

◆ Use a recipe that uses food exchanged when the two worlds met.
◆ Display other foods that were exchanged but not to be eaten at the feast.
◆ Display pictures of food that were exchanged.

The Columbus Encounter © 1992 Zephyr Press, Tucson, AZ

CROSSWORD KEY

The Columbus Encounter © 1992 Zephyr Press, Tucson, AZ

BIBLIOGRAPHY

BOOKS AND VIDEOS FOR TEACHERS

Caduto, M., and J. Bruchac. *Keepers of the Earth: Native American Stories and Environmental Activities for Children*. Golden, Colorado: Fulcrum, 1988. An interdisciplinary approach to exploring the Earth and Native American cultures. Legends, myths, folklore, and engaging activities. Promotes a sense of the unity of all life.

1492–1992—When Worlds Collide: How Columbus's Voyages Transformed Both East and West. *Newsweek*, Columbus Special Issue, Fall/Winter 1991. A joint project with the Smithsonian Natural History exhibit *Seeds of Change*. Many good articles on this topic. Be aware that there are graphic drawings of torture from Columbus's time (p. 51) and mistreatment of slaves (p. 69).

Herman, Viola. *After Columbus: The Smithsonian Chronicle; Teachers of the North American Indian*. Washington, D.C.: Smithsonian Books, 1990. Photos and text trace the fate of the Native Americans from the earliest contact with Europeans to the present.

Herman, Viola, and Carolyn Margolis. *Seeds of Change: A Quincentennial Commemoration*. Washington, D.C.: Smithsonian Institution Press, 1991. Discusses the plant, animal, and disease exchanges of both worlds in 1492 and how they affect us today.

Johnson, M., D. Yakubu, and B. Wass. *African Cultural Heritage*. 4-H Leader Guide, no. 399A. Order for $10.00 each from Director, Cooperative Extension Services, Michigan State University, East Lansing, MI 48824.

Public Broadcasting System. *Columbus and the Age of Discovery*. Seven one-hour videos portray an elaborate visual history. The Native American viewpoint is not fully developed.

Rethinking Columbus. Special edition of *Rethinking Schools*, 1991. 96 pages. K–College. $4.00 from Rethinking Schools, 1001 E. Keefe Ave., Milwaukee, WI 53212. Represents Native American points of view.

STUDENT REFERENCES

Note to the teacher: This list includes references for all sections. As some materials are controversial, we have tried to include those that are most balanced in presenting a worldview and that tell a more "complete" story of Columbus's impact on Native America instead of ending when he first steps on land.

Teachers should be aware that some *adult* books on Columbus display graphic woodcuts of Native Americans having hands and noses chopped off and being burned alive as well as enduring other torture. *If you use adult books, please preview carefully.*

Who "Discovered" America

Batherman, Muriel. *Before Columbus*. Houghton, 1981. Describes hunters, basket makers and farmers who lived in America thousands of years ago. Includes information about where they came from. (K–3)

Jackson, D. D. "Who the Heck Did Discover the New World?" *Smithsonian*, vol. 22 (6), September 1991. pp.76–85. (4–8)

Leon, George de Lucenary. *Explorers of the Americas Before Columbus*. Watts, 1989. Expertly traces lines of early voyagers. (4–8)

Maestro, Betsy, and Guilio Maestro. *The Discovery of the Americas*. Lothrop, Lee, Shepard, 1991. Discusses both hypothetical and historical voyages to America by the Phoenicians, St. Brenden of Ireland, the Vikings, Columbus, John Cabot, and Ferdinand Magellan. (K–3)

Simon, Charnan. *Leif Eriksson and the Vikings*. Children's Press, 1991. Full-color illustrations. (4–8)

"Who Came to America Before Columbus?" *Cobblestone Magazine*, October, 1984. Entire issue covers many explorers. Discusses modern archaeological techniques. (4–8)

Christopher Columbus

Adler, David A. *A First Biography: Christopher Columbus Great Explorer*. New York: Holiday House, 1991. Chronicles the life, voyages, and discoveries of the explorer. Uses the term Indians rather than Native Americans. (3–5)

Conrad, Pam. *Pedro's Journal: A Voyage with Christopher Columbus*. Boyds Mills Press/Caroline House, 1991. Written as a diary by the ship's boy, this story presents a personal view of Columbus's first voyage across the Atlantic. Pedro is chosen to go because he can read and write and Columbus thought he might be useful. (3–6)

Fischetto, Laura. *All Pigs on Deck: Christopher Columbus's Second Marvelous Voyage*. Delacorte Press, 1991. Relates the events of Columbus's second voyage focusing on the arrival of pigs in the Americas. A rollicking picture book, it depicts the idea of a "colony." Some things and ways of doing things from Europe didn't work in the Americas. The author's note mentions Columbus's harsh treatment of Native Americans and subsequent removal from office as governor. (K–3)

Haskins, Jim. *Christopher Columbus, Admiral of the Ocean Sea*. Scholastic Inc., 1990. Well-documented bibliography, often notes modern archaeological practices to deduce information. (5–8)

Leistman, Vicki. *Columbus Day*. Carolrhoda Books, 1991. Discusses the treatment of Native Americans. Balanced view. Educates children as to Columbus myth. Includes short history of Columbus Day. (K–3)

Levinson, Nancy S. *Christopher Columbus: Voyager to the Unknown*. Lodestar, 1990. Good discussion of the facts and myths. Lists crew on the three ships and gives chronology of events. (4–8)

Meltzer, Milton. *Columbus and the World Around Him*. Franklin Watts, 1990. Describes voyages of Columbus, the terrible impact of the Spaniards on the native peoples, and the cultural influences of the Native Americans on the white conquerors. (6 and up)

Roop, Peter, and Connie Roop, eds. *I, Columbus: My Journal—1492–93*. Walker, 1990. The authors have taken passages from Columbus's log to tell the story of the 1492 journey. (4–7)

Ventura, Piero. *Christopher Columbus*. New York: Random House, 1978. A brief biography highlighting his voyages. Detailed illustrations of Native American life at this time. Section on "a world of new plants." Does not mention his mistreatment of Native Americans. (K–3)

The World in 1492: *The Americas*

Bateman, Penny. *Great Civilizations: Aztecs and Incas* A.D. *1300–1532*. New York: Franklin Watts, 1988. Covers development of both civilizations; includes drawings, maps, diagrams, and photos. (4–6)

Batherman, Muriel. *Before Columbus*. Houghton Mifflin, 1990. Describes dwellings, tools, daily life of the earliest peoples. Based on archaeological findings. (K–3)

Brother Eagle, Sister Sky: A Message from Chief Seattle. Dial, 1991. Chief Seattle's moving, poignant message stunningly illustrated. Everyone, young and old, should read this. (K and up)

Fisher, Leonard Everett. *Pyramid of the Sun, Pyramid of the Moon*. Macmillan, 1988. Starkly dramatic black and white paintings and concise text tell about the pyramids built by the Teotihuacans in ancient Mexico. Discusses Toltec, Chichicmec, and Aztec civilizations, and the invasion of Cortez. (4–8)

"1491 America Before Columbus." *National Geographic* October 1991, pp. 4–99. See also the other series on Columbus and the Americas in *National Geographic*.

Freedman, R. *Buffalo Hunt*. New York: Holiday House, 1988. Examines the importance of the buffalo to Plains Indians. Describes hunting methods and the uses found for each part of the animal that could not be eaten. (4–8)

Freedman, R. *Indian Chiefs*. New York: Holiday House, 1987. The story of the decline of the Native Americans as seen through the eyes of great Indian leaders. (4–8)

Glubok, Shirley. *The Art of Ancient Peru*. Harper and Row, 1966. Photos and text depict art works of early cultures from the Chavan, Mochica, Nasca, and Tiahuanaco to the Chimu and Inca Empires, a span of 2000 years. (K–3)

History of the World: Civilizations of the Americas. Milwaukee: Rountree Publishers, 1989. Describes the early civilizations of North, Central, and South America through the time of Columbus. Excellent drawings, maps, artifacts, diagrams. Brief summaries of each civilization. (4–7)

The Indian Book. 1980 Childcraft Annual. World Book-Childcraft International, 1980. Thirteen Native American tribes from North and South America are discussed. Discusses who they were, where they came from, how they lived. Very comprehensive. Drawings as well as photos of artifacts. Includes legends and myths. Crafts. (4–7)

Miles, Miska. *Annie and the Old One*. Little Brown, 1971. A contemporary Navajo grandmother teaches her granddaughter Navajo traditions and weaving. (4–8)

Odijk, Pamela. *The Aztecs*. Silver Burdett Press, 1989. Surveys the culture, government, religion, and achievements of the Aztecs and the collapse of their empire with the arrival of the Spanish under Cortez. Uses photos and drawings of art and land. Discusses Aztec human sacrifice. Section on Aztec inventions and special skills. (4–8)

Ortiz, S. *The People Shall Continue*. Children's Press, 1987. A Native American perspective of their history and their country's invasion by Europeans. Storytelling format stresses the unity of all life and need for people to work together to safeguard life on earth. (4–8)

Pitkanen, Matti. *Grandchildren of the Incas*. Carolrhoda, 1991. A photo essay describes the civilization of the ancient Incas comparing it to the lifestyles of their modern descendants, the Quechua Indians of Peru. (K–3)

Sewell, Marcia. *People of the Breaking Day*. New York: Atheneum, 1990. Re-creates the world of the Wampanoagas. A poetic presentation of their traditions. (K–3)

The World in 1492: *Africa*

Addison, John. *Ancient Africa*. John Day Co., 1970. Introduces the reader to Africa's ancient states. Factual reference. (7 and up)

The Asante World. *Faces: The Magazine about People*. January 1985. The entire issue covers the Asante culture, art, and customs; includes a game. (4–8)

Feelings, Muriel. *Jambo Means Hello*. Dial Press. Many Swahili words help give a feeling for African culture and tradition. Illustrations enhance the text. (K–3)

Glubok, Shirley. *Art of Africa*. Harper and Row, 1965. Photos and descriptive text of masks, carvings, sculpture, rock painting, woven baskets, and other artifacts. (K–3)

Grifalconi, Ann. *The Village of Round and Square Houses*. Little Brown, 1986. A young girl listens to the story of why men live in square houses while women live in round houses. Each has a place to be apart and a time to be together. Respect for the wisdom of others is featured. Bold illustrations. (K–3)

Madagascar. *Faces: The Magazine about People*. March, 1989. Issue covers their culture, including a recipe, game, folktales, and history. (4–8)

Mursky, Reba Paeff. *Thirty-one Brothers and Sisters*. Dell, 1952. A fascinating account of daily life in the veld. Nomusa, daughter of a Zulu Chief, loves all her little brothers and sisters and enjoys helping to care for them. However, she longs to go on an elephant hunt, a privilege reserved for men and boys. How she gets her wish is a fascinating adventure. (4–8)

Musgrove, Margaret. *Ashanti to Zulu: African Traditions*. Dial Press, 1976. Explains some traditions and customs of 26 African tribes beginning with the letters A through Z. (K–3)

South Africa. *Faces: The Magazine about People*. January 1991. Entire issue examines South African history and culture. (4–8)

Steptoe, John. *Mufaro's Beautiful Daughters: An African Tale*. Lothrop, Lee, Shepard, 1987. Two beautiful daughters compete for the king's attention when he announces that he is looking for a wife. Beautiful illustrations rich in detail on the region of ancient Zimbabwe. Reading Rainbow feature book. (K–3)

The World in 1492: *The Orient*

Beshore, George. *Science in Ancient China*. Franklin Watts, 1988. Surveys the achievements of the ancient Chinese in science, medicine, astronomy, and cosmology, and describes such innovations as rockets, wells, the compass, water wheels, and movable type. (4–8)

Borja, Robert, and Corinne Borja. *Making Chinese Papercuts*. Albert Whitman, 1980. Highlights the origins and uses of Chinese papercutting and presents instructions for projects. (4–8)

Cox, David. *Ayu and the Perfect Moon*. London: Bodley Head, 1983. On the exotic island of Bali, Ayu tells her young friends how she once performed a magnificent dance under the light of the full moon. (K–3)

Fisher, Leonard Everett. *The Great Wall of China*. Macmillan, 1986. A brief history of the Great Wall of China, begun about 2,200 years ago to keep out Mongol invaders. (K–3)

Haskins, Jim. *Count Your Way Through China*. Carolrhoda, 1987. Counts from one to ten in Chinese calligraphy. Each number ties in with a description of some aspect of Chinese life and cultures. (K–3)

Heyer, Marilee. *The Weaving of a Dream: A Chinese Folktale*. Viking Kestrel, 1986. When the beautiful tapestry woven by a poor woman is stolen by fairies, her three sons set out on a magical journey to retrieve it. Elegant illustrations decorate this tale. (4–8)

Ludwig, Lyndell. *How to Weigh an Elephant: An Ancient Chinese Folktale*. Donald S. Ellis, 1983. A foreign prince sends an elephant as a gift to a Chinese lord. The people of Wei kingdom have never seen an elephant! The Chinese lord, amazed by its size, would like it weighed. The merchants tell him there are no scales large enough. Finally, the lord's son solves the problem. (K–3)

Williams, Jay. *Everyone Knows What a Dragon Looks Like*. Four Winds, 1976. Only the coming of a true dragon can save a Chinese kingdom from northern invaders. When a funny, fat old man shows up claiming to be a dragon, no one believes him but a poor, young boy. (K–3)

The World in 1492: *Renaissance Europe*

Caselli, Giovanni. *The Renaissance and the New World*. New York: Peter Bedrick Bks, 1986. Very detailed diagrams of many aspects of everyday life. (4–8)

Harris, Nathaniel. *Leonardo and the Renaissance*. New York: Bookwright Press, 1987. (4–8)

Middleton, Haydn. *Everyday Life in the Sixteenth Century*. Silver Burdett Co., 1982. Covers the many aspects of living in the Renaissance era. (4–7)

Raboff, Ernest. *Michelangelo*. Harper & Row, 1988. Brief biography of Michelangelo. Fourteen color reproductions and critical interpretation of his works. (3–6)

Venezia, Mike. *Da Vinci*. Children's Press, 1989. Traces the life of the Renaissance artist and analyzes some of his paintings. (2–4)

Ventura, Piero. *Michelangelo's World*. G.P. Putnam, 1988. Recounts the life of the famous sculptor, painter poet, and architect. Told in the first person as if by Michelangelo himself. (3–6)

Exploration of the 1400s and 1500s

Ceserani, Gran Paolo. *Marco Polo*. Italy, New York: Putnam's Sons, 1977, 1982. Detailed illustrations show thirteenth-century life along Marco Polo's route of travel. Text discusses travels; illustrations depict architecture, dress, and daily activities. One could study the illustrations for hours. (2–5)

Fisher, Leonard E. *Prince Henry, the Navigator*. MacMillan, 1990. Picture book biography of Portuguese prince whose early school of navigation affected late explorers. (2–6)

Kramer, Ann, and Simon Adams. *Historical Atlas: Exploration and Empire, Empire-builders, European Expansion and Development of Science*. Warwick Press, 1989. Describes historical and social events in various nations during the period of exploration from 1450 to 1760. Includes maps, charts, diagrams, photos, and contemporary drawings. (4–8)

Matthews, Rupert. *Explorers*. Eyewitness Books. New York: Alfred A. Knopf, 1991. A photo essay about ancient to modern explorations of the land, sea, and space. Has a section on the Chinese and Arabs not easily found elsewhere. (4–8)

Poole, Frederick King. *Early Explorations of North America*. Watts, 1989. Includes Vikings, early Spanish and French adventurers. (3–5)

Reynolds, Kathy. *Marco Polo*. Raintree Children's Books, 1986. Told as if Marco Polo were recounting his journey. (4–8)

Rosen, Mike. *The Travels of Marco Polo*. New York: Bookwright Press, 1989. Traces the journeys and discoveries of the thirteenth-century Italian merchant. Includes maps, photos, and drawings. Presents both positive and negative aspects of Kublai Khan's Court. Good coverage of life at the time. (4–8)

500 Years of Change

Aliki. *Corn Is Maize: The Gift of the Indian*. Thomas Y. Crowell, 1976. How Indian farmers long ago found a wild grass plant, made it an important part of their lives, learned the best ways to grow it, and shared it with the new settlers of America. (K–3)

"1492–1992—When Worlds Collide: How Columbus's Voyages Transformed Both East and West." *Newsweek*, Columbus Special Issue, Fall/Winter 1991. A joint project with the Smithsonian natural history exhibit *Seeds of Change*. Many good articles on this topic. Be aware that there is a graphic drawing of torture from Columbus's time (p. 51) and mistreatment of slaves (p. 69). (4–8)

Hudson, Jan. *Sweet Grass*. Philomel, 1989. Set among the Blackfeet of nineteenth-century Canada, tells of the devastation of a smallpox epidemic brought to a young girl's tribe by white settlers. (6–8)

Jurmain, Suzanne. *Once Upon a Horse: A History of Horses and How They Shaped our History*. Lolhrop, 1989. Well illustrated. (5–8)

Linden, Eugene. Lost Tribes, Lost Knowledge: When Native Cultures Disappear, So Does a Trove of Scientific and Medical Wisdom. *Time* September 23, 1991, pp. 46–56. (4–8)

Macaulay, David. *Motel of the Mysteries*. Houghten Mifflin, 1979. An archaeological spoof. In the future, a team of archaeologists uncovers a twentieth-century motel and deduces what our everyday items were used for. Hilarious! Shows how easy it is to misinterpret history. (4–8)

Poatgieter, Hermina. *Indian Legacy: Native American Influences on World Life and Culture*. New York: Julian Messner, 1981. Discusses the important contributions made by the Native Americans of North and South America throughout the world. (6 and up)

Turner, Dorothy. *Potatoes*. Minneapolis, Carolrhoda, 1988. Describes the history, cultivation, and nutritional values of the potato. Includes recipes, instructions for making potato prints, and tips on how to grow your own potatoes. (K–3)

Zephyr Learning Packets

Humanities & Social Studies Series

You'll learn with *Zephyr Learning Packets* along with your students! That's what teachers say about this best-selling series. These interdisciplinary research-based packets are just what the teacher ordered to inspire every kid in the classroom!

Here are 25 jam-packed activity units that promote critical and creative thinking and provide students with hands-on problem-solving, research, and higher-level thinking skills. Students discover the excitement of self-directed study with these absorbing topics. The best part ... you facilitate the process and your students do the learning.

The Learning Packets —
- Are reproducible for each student
- Require student research and reporting
- Promote critical and creative thinking
- Need little teacher preparation or supervision
- Are easy to use

Each Packet Includes —
- Interdisciplinary and integrative activities
- Complete bibliography
- Art exploration section
- Learning center ideas
- Two units: K-3 & 4-8

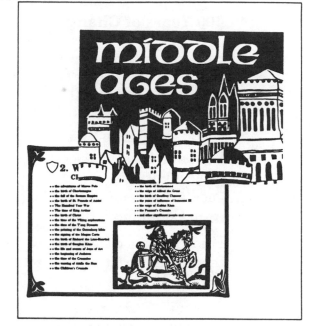

NEW!
The Blue and the Gray
America's Civil War (1861-1865)
by Carol Hauswald and Earl Bitoy (1992)
Your students will explore the causes and effects of the American Civil War, the war that forged our *United States*. This high-interest unit promotes independent discovery as well as learning-center/task-card activities for cooperative learning.
ZP20-W $19.95

Early People
by Beaham and Tanner (1983)
Students uncover the mysteries of early people and culture. They'll research the discovery of fire, the development of tools, weapons, and agriculture in the context of the Pleistocene, Paleolithic, Mesolithic, and Neolithic periods.
ZP06-W $19.95

Wassily Kandinsky
by Stephany Grassinger (1980)
Kids love Kandinsky because his style is much fun to recreate. They'll share his love of color and shape as they explore the artist's perspective and his stylistic development.
ZM05-W $19.95

NEW!
Jade Garden
Ancient to Modern China
by Carol Hauswald and Earl Bitoy (1991)
Open the door to the study of Chinese culture with the innovative activities in this new *Zephyr Learning Packet*. With its romantic past and ever-changing present, the study of China has never been more timely.
ZP19-W $19.95

Middle Ages
by Joey Tanner (1981)
Crusade through time as students investigate the Dark Ages and create a time line through the birth of Christ through the reign of Kublai Khan.
ZP07-W $19.95

Old Russia 1400-1917
by Dianne Jones (1989)
Step back in time, beginning with the Mir to Imperial Russia — the czars, the cossacks, the Bolshevik Revolution. Students research Tchaikovsky, the Bolshoi Ballet and Opera, and the Mongolian Invasions.
ZP17-W $19.95

The Renaissance 1300 – 1600 A.D.
Man, The Measure of All Things
by Jennifer Moreland (1988)
Students connect the past and present as they venture into this inspirational era. And they'll learn about such fascinating people as Leonardo da Vinci, Johann Gutenberg, and Martin Luther.
ZP08-W $19.95

American History
by Gaeel Beaham (1983)
Climb aboard the wagon train west with this inquiry into the concepts and ideas that built America.
ZM01-W $19.95

The Americas
by Gaeel Beaham
A look at the Americas' pre-history — the development of agricultural societies, the purpose of a family, and the migration of early people. Students probe early cultures of Alaskan Eskimos, Mayans, and Incas and then present their findings in time lines, dioramas, creative writing, and more.
ZP01-W $19.95

Ancient Civilizations
by Clements, Domin, and Tanner (1983)
Send your students back in a time machine to the ancient Middle Eastern civilizations. They'll research economic and educational systems, including the alphabet, mathematics, and applied sciences.
ZP02-W $19.95

Early Japan
by Ruth Patzman (1983)
Say "sayonara" to boring research! Students take a look at the fascinating rituals of Japanese history.
ZP05-W $19.95

Ancient Greece and Rome
by Clements, Domin, and Tanner (1983)
The development of art and science in this noble empire created the cultural and intellectual center of its time.
ZP04-W $19.95

Ancient Egypt
by Clements, Domin, and Tanner (1983)
Your students discover the majesty of the Pharoahs, pyramids, hieroglyphics, the arts, and more.
ZP03-W $19.95

The Industrial Revolution of the Nineteenth Century
by Jennifer Moreland (1990)
Your students will explore this significant era in world history. They will study the social events and the technological and medical wonders that have changed the way we live.
ZP18-W $19.95

Zephyr Press
3316 N. Chapel Ave. • P.O. Box 13448-W
Tucson, Arizona 85732-3448 • (602) 322-5090

See Zephyr Learning Packets – Science Series for Special Quantity Discounts Offer on all Zephyr Learning Packets →

Zephyr Learning Packets
Science Series

These self-directed study units are flexible. You can select one subject for the entire class — or offer several closely related topics like Paleontology, Archaeology, and the Americas and students can choose their favorite. Copy the selected unit and conference with each student and let the research begin! Within the structure of each unit, students are given opportunities to —

- Make choices
- Learn at their own pace
- Learn in a manner more closely suited to their own learning styles
- Expand research skills
- Use a variety of modalities
- Plan their own time
- Develop creative and critical thinking skills
- Experience whole-brain learning

Futuristics
by Joey Tanner (revised 1992)
Your students will analyze trends, make predictions, and plan creatively to provide direction for our future. A favorite of forward-thinking educators.
ZM03-W $19.95

NEW!
Rocks and Minerals
The Earth's Natural Wonders
by Carol Hauswald (1992)
Rock hounds unite! Explore the wonders of those materials that are the earth's building blocks. Take your students' understanding of rocks even further by integrating this unit with *Volcanology* and *Paleontology*.
ZP21-W $19.95

Volcanology
by Bonnie Rasmussen (1983)
An eruption of learning — the facts as well as the legends and myths surrounding volcanoes.
ZP16-W $19.95

Paleontology
by Joey Tanner (1983)
Kids of all ages love dinosaurs! Catch the craze with this instantly interesting unit as they unearth extinct plants and animals, piecing together parts of a puzzle missing for millions of years.
ZP15-W $19.95

Ecology
Learning to Love Our Planet
by Susan Diffenderfer (1984)
Our planet's future depends on our children. This unit helps develop and expand their awareness of what people can do to create a healthier world.
ZP11-W $19.95

Entomology
by Clements, Domin, and Tanner (1983)
Eeeuooo! Students buzz with knowledge as they classify, collect, observe, and identify some of the 900,000 species of the insect kingdom.
ZP12-W $19.95

Science Fiction
by Patricia Payson (1980)
Imaginations run wild with this delightful literature unit. Students take a peek at cloning, robotics, body freezing, and other cosmic possibilities.
ZM04-W $19.95

Marine Biology
by Joey Tanner (revised 1992)
Dive into the ecology of the sea. Students study the delicate relationships between the organisms that make up food chains and the mysteries of the ocean floor.
ZP14-W $19.95

Astronomy
by Carolyn Zolg (1981)
This galactic unit goes light years beyond the typical look at the planets and galaxies with projects like building a telescope or sundial, designing a model of the solar system, and creating a constellation show.
ZP10-W $19.95

Archaeology
by Joey Tanner (1981)
Students uncover geologic history, artifacts, and finds as they research "found" cultures, compare and contrast religions of ancient civilizations, and create a mural of Atlantis.
ZP09-W $19.95

Geology
Our Changing Earth
by Diffenderfer, Zolg, and Tanner (1983)
Students unearth creative and critical thinking as they research plate tectonics, magnetic poles, potential energy sources from the ocean, groundwater and its pollution, controversies in river use, and careers in geology.
ZP13-W $19.95

Zephyr Press
3316 N. Chapel Ave. • P.O. Box 13448-W
Tucson, Arizona 85732-3448 • (602) 322-5090